D0286400

Key Element Guide
ITIL® Continual Service Improvement

London: TSO

⊠ TSO

information & publishing solutions

Published by TSO (The Stationery Office) and available from:

Online
www.tsoshop.co.uk

Mail, Telephone, Fax & E-mail
TSO
PO Box 29, Norwich, NR3 1GN
Telephone orders/General enquiries:
0870 600 5522
Fax orders: 0870 600 5533
E-mail: customer.services@tso.co.uk
Textphone 0870 240 3701

TSO@Blackwell and other Accredited Agents

First edition Crown copyright 2008
Second edition Crown copyright 2012

Third impression 2014

ISBN 9780113313648 (Single copy ISBN)
ISBN 9780113313693 (Sold in a pack of 10 copies)

Printed in the United Kingdom for The Stationery Office

Material is FSC certified and produced using ECF pulp, sourced from fully sustainable forests.

P002500752 c18   07/12

Contents

Acknowledgements

AUTHOR
Vernon Lloyd, Fox IT

KEY ELEMENT GUIDE AUTHORING TEAM
David Cannon, BMC Software

Ashley Hanna, HP

Lou Hunnebeck, Third Sky Inc.

Stuart Rance, HP

Randy Steinberg, Migration Technologies Inc.

REVIEWERS
Best Management Practice and The Stationery Office would like to thank itSMF International for managing the quality assurance of this publication, and the following reviewers for their contributions:

Duncan Anderson, Global Knowledge; John Donoghue, Allied Irish Bank plc; John Earle, itSMF Ireland Ltd; Robert Falkowitz, Concentric Circle Consulting; Padraig Farrell, SureSkills; Siobhan Flaherty, Generali PanEurope; Signe Marie Hernes Bjerke, Det Norske Veritas; Michael Imhoff Nielsen, IBM; Jackie Manning, Bord Gáis Networks; Krikor Maroukian, King's College London; Reiko Morita, Ability InterBusiness Solutions, Inc.; Trevor Murray, The Grey Matters; Gary O'Dwyer, Allied Irish Banks plc; Benjamin Orazem, SRC d.o.o.; Sue Shaw, TriCentrica; Marco Smith, iCore Ltd; Hon P Suen, ECT Service Ltd; and Paul Wigzel, Paul Wigzel Training and Consultancy.

1   Introduction

This key element guide is intended to provide a summary of the basic concepts and practice elements of *ITIL Continual Service Improvement*, which forms part of the core ITIL publication suite.

ITIL is a set of best-practice publications for IT service management (ITSM).[1] ITIL provides guidance on the provision of quality IT services, and on the capabilities needed to support them. ITIL is not a standard that has to be followed; it is guidance that should be read and understood, and used to create value for the service provider and its customers. Organizations are encouraged to adopt ITIL best practices and to adapt them to work in their specific environments in ways that meet their needs.

ITIL is the most widely recognized framework for ITSM in the world. In the 20 years since it was created, ITIL has evolved and changed its breadth and depth as technologies and business practices have developed.

The section numbering in this key element guide is not the same as the section numbers in the core publication, *ITIL Continual Service Improvement*. Therefore, do not try to use references to section numbers in the core publication when referencing material in this key element guide.

1.1   THE ITIL SERVICE LIFECYCLE

The ITIL framework is based on five stages of the service lifecycle as shown in Figure 1.1, with a core publication providing

---

[1] ITSM and other concepts from this chapter are described in more detail in Chapter 2.

Figure 1.1 The ITIL service lifecycle

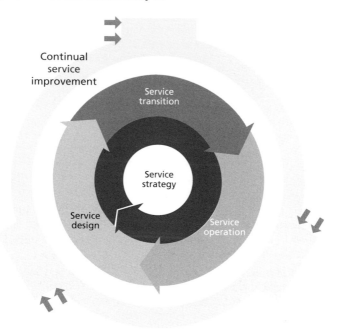

best-practice guidance for each stage. This guidance includes principles, processes and activities, organization and roles, technology, challenges, critical success factors, and risks. The service lifecycle uses a hub-and-spoke design, with service strategy at the hub, and service design, service transition and service operation as the revolving lifecycle stages or 'spokes'.

Continual service improvement surrounds and supports all stages of the service lifecycle. Each stage of the lifecycle exerts influence on the others and relies on them for inputs and feedback. In this way, a constant set of checks and balances ensures that as business demand changes, the services can adapt and respond effectively.

In addition to the core publications, there is also a complementary set of ITIL publications providing guidance specific to industry sectors, organization types, operating models and technology architectures.

The following key characteristics of ITIL contribute to its global success:

- **Vendor-neutral** ITIL service management practices are not based on any particular technology platform or industry type. ITIL is owned by the UK government and is not tied to any commercial proprietary practice or solution.
- **Non-prescriptive** ITIL offers robust, mature and time-tested practices that have applicability to all types of service organization. It continues to be useful and relevant in public and private sectors, internal and external service providers, small, medium and large enterprises, and within any technical environment.
- **Best practice** ITIL represents the learning experiences and thought leadership of the world's best-in-class service providers.

1.2   CONTINUAL SERVICE IMPROVEMENT – KEY ELEMENT GUIDE

ITIL Continual Service Improvement provides best-practice guidance for the continual service improvement (CSI) stage of the service lifecycle.

1.2.1   Purpose and objectives of CSI

The purpose of the CSI stage is to align IT services with changing business needs by identifying improvements that are required to the IT services that support business processes. These improvement activities support the lifecycle approach through service strategy, service design, service transition and service operation. CSI is always seeking ways to improve service effectiveness, process effectiveness and cost effectiveness.

The objectives of CSI are to:

- Review, analyse, prioritize and make recommendations on improvement opportunities in each lifecycle stage
- Review and analyse service level achievement to identify areas requiring improvement
- Identify and help to implement specific activities to improve IT service quality and improve the efficiency and effectiveness of the enabling processes
- Improve the cost effectiveness of delivering IT services without sacrificing customer satisfaction
- Ensure that applicable quality management methods are used to support continual improvement activities
- Ensure that processes have clearly defined objectives and measurements that lead to actionable improvements.

1.2.2 Scope

ITIL Continual Service Improvement provides guidance in four main areas:

- The overall health of ITSM as a discipline
- The continual alignment of the service portfolio with the current and future business needs
- The maturity and capability of the organization, management, processes and people utilized by the services
- Continual improvement of all aspects of the IT service and the service assets that support them.

The following activities support CSI:

- Reviewing management information and trends to ensure that services are meeting agreed service levels, and that the output of the enabling processes are achieving the desired results
- Conducting service reviews and assessments generally to identify potential areas for improvement
- Periodically conducting internal audits verifying process compliance
- Reviewing existing deliverables for appropriateness
- Periodically conducting customer satisfaction surveys
- Reviewing business trends and changed priorities, and keeping abreast of business projections
- Measuring and identifying the value created by CSI improvements.

The deliverables of CSI must be reviewed on an ongoing basis to verify completeness, functionality and feasibility and to ensure that they remain relevant and usable.

1.2.3   Value to business

Adopting and implementing standard and consistent approaches for CSI will:

■ Lead to a gradual and continual improvement in service quality
■ Ensure that IT services remain continuously aligned to business requirements
■ Result in gradual improvements in cost effectiveness through a reduction in costs and/or the capability to handle more work at the same cost
■ Use monitoring and reporting to identify opportunities for improvement in all lifecycle stages and in all processes
■ Identify opportunities for improvements in organizational structures, resourcing capabilities, partners, technology, staff skills and training, and communications.

1.3   CONTEXT

Each core ITIL publication addresses those capabilities that have a direct impact on a service provider's performance. The core is expected to provide structure, stability and strength to service management capabilities, with durable principles, methods and tools. This serves to protect investments and provide the necessary basis for measurement, learning and improvement.

1.3.1   Service strategy

At the centre of the service lifecycle is service strategy. Value creation begins here with understanding organizational objectives and customer needs. Every organizational asset, including people, processes and products, should support the strategy.

ITIL Service Strategy provides guidance on how to view service management not only as an organizational capability but as a strategic asset. It describes the principles underpinning the practice of service management which are useful for developing service management policies, guidelines and processes across the service lifecycle.

Organizations already practising ITIL can use *ITIL Service Strategy* to guide a strategic review of their service management capabilities and to improve the alignment between those capabilities and their business strategies. *ITIL Service Strategy* will encourage readers to stop and think about *why* something is to be done before thinking of *how*.

1.3.2   Service design

Service design is the stage in the lifecycle that turns a service strategy into a plan for delivering business objectives. *ITIL Service Design* provides guidance for the design and development of services and service management practices. It covers design principles and methods for converting strategic objectives into portfolios of services and service assets. The scope of *ITIL Service Design* includes the changes and improvements necessary to increase or maintain value to customers over the lifecycle of services, the continuity of services, the achievement of service levels, and conformance to standards and regulations.

1.3.3   Service transition

ITIL Service Transition provides guidance for the development and improvement of capabilities for introducing new and changed services into supported environments. It describes how to transition an organization from one state to another while controlling risk and supporting organizational knowledge for decision support. It ensures that the value(s) identified in the service strategy, and encoded in the service design, are effectively transitioned so that they can be realized in service operation.

1.3.4   Service operation

ITIL Service Operation describes best practice for managing services in supported environments. It includes guidance on achieving effectiveness and efficiency in the delivery and support of services to ensure value for the customer, the users and the service provider. *ITIL Service Operation* provides guidance on how to maintain stability in service operation, even while allowing for changes in design, scale, scope and service levels.

1.3.5   Continual service improvement

ITIL Continual Service Improvement provides guidance on creating and maintaining value for customers through better strategy, design, transition and operation of services. It combines principles, practices and methods from quality management, change management and capability improvement.

ITIL Continual Service Improvement describes best practice for achieving incremental and large-scale improvements in service quality, operational efficiency and business continuity, and for ensuring that the service portfolio continues to be aligned to business needs.

2   Service management as a practice

2.1   SERVICES AND SERVICE MANAGEMENT

2.1.1   Services

Definitions

Service: A means of delivering value to customers by facilitating outcomes customers want to achieve without the ownership of specific costs and risks.

IT service: A service provided by an IT service provider. An IT service is made up of a combination of information technology, people and processes. A customer-facing IT service directly supports the business processes of one or more customers and its service level targets should be defined in a service level agreement. Other IT services, called supporting services, are not directly used by the business but are required by the service provider to deliver customer-facing services.

Outcome: The result of carrying out an activity, following a process, or delivering an IT service etc. The term is used to refer to intended results, as well as to actual results.

An outcome-based definition of service moves IT organizations beyond business–IT alignment towards business–IT integration. Customers seek outcomes but do not wish to have accountability or ownership of all the associated costs and risks. The customer can judge the value of a service based on a comparison of cost or price and reliability with the desired outcome. Customer satisfaction is also important. Customer expectations keep shifting, and a service provider that does not track this will soon lose business.

2.1.2   Service management

Business would like IT services to behave like other utilities such as water, electricity or the telephone. Simply having the best technology does not ensure that the IT service will provide utility-like reliability. Service management can bring this utility quality of service to the business.

> **Definitions**
>
> *Service management*: A set of specialized organizational capabilities for providing value to customers in the form of services.
>
> *Service provider*: An organization supplying services to one or more internal or external customers.

The more mature a service provider's capabilities are, the greater is their ability to meet the needs of the customer. The act of transforming capabilities and resources into valuable services is at the core of service management. The origins of service management are in traditional service businesses such as airlines, banks and hotels.

2.1.3   IT service management

Every IT organization should act as a service provider, using service management to ensure that they deliver outcomes required by their customers. A service level agreement (SLA) is used to document agreements between an IT service provider and a customer. An SLA describes the service, documents targets, and specifies the responsibilities of the service provider and the customer.

2.1.4   Service providers

There are three main types of service provider:

- **Type I – internal service provider** This type is embedded within a business unit. There may be several Type I service providers within an organization.
- **Type II – shared services unit** An internal service provider that provides shared IT services to more than one business unit.
- **Type III – external service provider** A service provider that provides IT services to external customers.

IT service management (ITSM) concepts are often described in the context of only one of these types. In reality most organizations have a combination of IT service provider types.

2.1.5   Stakeholders in service management

Stakeholders have an interest in an organization, project or service etc. and may also be interested in the activities, targets, resources or deliverables. There are many stakeholders inside the service provider. There are also many external stakeholders, for example:

- **Customers** Those who buy goods or services. Customers define and agree the service level targets.
- **Users** Those who use the service on a day-to-day basis.
- **Suppliers** Third parties responsible for supplying goods or services that are required to deliver IT services.

There is a difference between internal customers and external customers:

■ **Internal customers** These work for the same business as the service provider – for example, the marketing department uses IT services.
■ **External customers** These work for a different business from the service provider. External customers typically purchase services by means of a legally binding contract or agreement.

2.1.6 Utility and warranty

From the customer's perspective, value consists of achieving business objectives. The value of a service is created by combining utility (fitness for purpose) and warranty (fitness for use).

■ **Utility** The ability to meet a particular need. It is often described as 'what the service does' – for example, a service that enables a business unit to process orders.
■ **Warranty** An assurance that the service will meet its agreed requirements. Warranty includes the ability of a service to be available when needed, to provide the required capacity, and to provide the required reliability in terms of continuity and security.

The value of a service is only created when both utility and warranty are designed and delivered.

Information about the desired business outcomes, opportunities, customers, utility and warranty of the service is used to develop the definition of a service. Using an outcome-based definition helps to ensure that managers plan and execute all aspects of service management from the customer's perspective.

2.1.7   Best practices in the public domain

Organizations benchmark themselves against peers and seek to close gaps in capabilities. This enables them to become more competitive. One way to close gaps is the adoption of best practices. There are several sources for best practice including public frameworks, standards and the proprietary knowledge of organizations and individuals. ITIL is the most widely recognized and trusted source of best-practice guidance for ITSM.

2.2   BASIC CONCEPTS

2.2.1   Assets, resources and capabilities

The relationship between service providers and customers revolves around the use of assets – both those of the service provider and those of the customer. The performance of customer assets is a primary concern for service management.

> **Definitions**
>
> *Asset*: Any resource or capability.
>
> *Customer asset*: Any resource or capability used by a customer to achieve a business outcome.
>
> *Service asset*: Any resource or capability used by a service provider to deliver services to a customer.

There are two types of asset – resources and capabilities. Resources are direct inputs for production. Capabilities represent an organization's ability to coordinate, control and deploy resources to produce value. It is relatively easy to acquire resources compared to capabilities. Figure 2.1 shows examples of capabilities and resources.

Figure 2.1 Examples of capabilities and resources

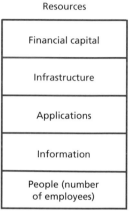

2.2.2   Processes

Definition: process

A process is a structured set of activities designed to accomplish a specific objective. A process takes one or more defined inputs and turns them into defined outputs.

Process characteristics include:

- **Measurability** We can measure the process in a relevant manner.
- **Specific results** The process delivers specific results, which must be individually identifiable and countable.

- ■ **Customers** The process delivers its primary results to a customer or stakeholder. Customers may be internal or external to the organization.
- ■ **Responsiveness to specific triggers** The process should be traceable to a specific trigger.

The outputs from the process should be driven by the process objectives. Process measurement and metrics can be built into the process to control and improve the process as illustrated in Figure 2.2.

Figure 2.2 Process model

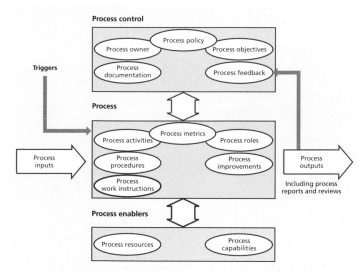

2.2.3 Organizing for service management

Best practices described in ITIL need to be tailored to suit organizations and situations. The starting point for organizational design is service strategy.

2.2.3.1 Functions

A function is a team or group of people and the tools or other resources they use to carry out one or more processes or activities. In larger organizations, a function may be performed by several departments, teams and groups. In smaller organizations, one person or group can perform multiple functions – for example, a technical management department could also incorporate the service desk function.

ITIL Service Operation describes the following functions:

- **Service desk** The single point of contact for users. A typical service desk manages incidents and service requests, and also handles communication with the users.
- **Technical management** Provides technical skills and resources needed to manage the IT infrastructure throughout the service lifecycle.
- **IT operations management** Executes the daily operational activities needed to manage IT services and the supporting IT infrastructure
- **Application management** Is responsible for managing applications throughout their lifecycle. This differs from application development which is mainly concerned with one-time activities for requirements, design and build of applications.

The other core ITIL publications rely on the technical and application management functions described in *ITIL Service Operation*, but they do not define any additional functions in detail.

2.2.3.2 Roles

The core ITIL publications provide guidelines and examples of role descriptions. In many cases roles will need to be combined or separated.

> **Definition: role**
>
> A role is a set of responsibilities, activities and authorities granted to a person or team. A role is defined in a process or function. One person or team may have multiple roles – for example, the roles of configuration manager and change manager may be carried out by a single person.

Roles are often confused with job titles but they are not the same. Each organization defines job titles and job descriptions, and individuals holding these job titles can perform one or more roles. See Chapter 5 for more details about roles and responsibilities.

2.2.4 The service portfolio

The service portfolio is the complete set of services managed by a service provider, and it represents the service provider's commitments and investments across all customers and market spaces. It consists of three parts:

- **Service pipeline** Services that are under consideration or development, but are not yet available to customers. The service pipeline is a service provider's business view of possible future services.
- **Service catalogue** Live IT services, including those available for deployment. It is the only part of the service portfolio that is published to customers. It includes a customer-facing view (or views) of the IT services. It also includes information about supporting services required by the service provider.
- **Retired services** Services that have retired.

Service providers often find it useful to distinguish customer-facing services from supporting services:

- **Customer-facing services** Visible to the customer. These normally support the customer's business processes and facilitate outcomes desired by the customer.
- **Supporting services** Support or 'underpin' the customer-facing services. These are typically invisible to the customer, but are essential to the delivery of customer-facing services.

Figure 2.3 illustrates the components of the service portfolio. These are important components of the service knowledge management system (SKMS) described in section 2.2.5.

2.2.5   Knowledge management and the SKMS

Knowledge and information enable people to perform activities and support information flow between lifecycle stages and processes. Implementing knowledge management enables effective decision support and reduces risks.

ITIL Service Transition describes an architecture for a service knowledge management system (SKMS) with four layers:

Figure 2.3 The service portfolio and its contents

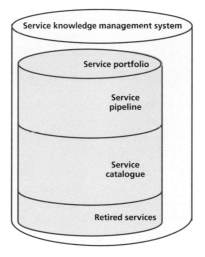

- ■ **Presentation layer** Enables searching, browsing, retrieving, updating, subscribing and collaboration. Different views are provided for different audiences.
- ■ **Knowledge-processing layer** Where information is converted into knowledge which enables decision-making.
- ■ **Information integration layer** Provides integrated information from data in multiple sources in the data layer.
- ■ **Data layer** Includes tools for data discovery and collection, and data items in unstructured and structured forms.

2.3   GOVERNANCE AND MANAGEMENT SYSTEMS

2.3.1   Governance

Governance defines the common directions, policies and rules that both the business and IT use to conduct business.

> **Definition: governance**
>
> Ensures that policies and strategy are actually implemented, and that required processes are correctly followed.
> Governance includes defining roles and responsibilities, measuring and reporting, and taking actions to resolve any issues identified.

Governance applies a consistently managed approach at all levels of the organization by ensuring a clear strategy is set, and by defining the policies needed to achieve the strategy.

2.3.2   Management systems

Many businesses have adopted management system standards for competitive advantage, to ensure a consistent approach in implementing service management, and to support governance.

An organization can adopt multiple management system standards, such as:

- A quality management system (ISO 9001)
- An environmental management system (ISO 14000)
- A service management system (ISO/IEC 20000)
- An information security management system (ISO/IEC 27001)
- A management system for software asset management (ISO/IEC 19770).

As there are common elements between such management systems, they should be managed in an integrated way rather than having separate management systems.

ISO management system standards use the Plan-Do-Check-Act (PDCA) cycle shown in Figure 2.4. This PDCA cycle is used in each of the core ITIL publications.

Figure 2.4 Plan-Do-Check-Act cycle

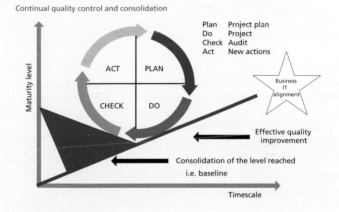

Definition: ISO/IEC 20000

An international standard for IT service management.

ISO/IEC 20000 is an international standard that allows organizations to prove best practice in ITSM. Part 1 specifies requirements for the service provider to plan, establish, implement, operate, monitor, review, maintain and improve a service management system (SMS). One of the most common routes for an organization to achieve the requirements of ISO/IEC 20000 is by adopting ITIL.

2.4   THE SERVICE LIFECYCLE

The service lifecycle is an organizing framework, supported by the organizational structure, service portfolio and service models within an organization. See Chapter 1 for an introduction to each ITIL service lifecycle stage.

2.4.1   Specialization and coordination across the lifecycle

Organizations should function in the same manner as a high-performing sports team. Each player in a team and each member of the team's organization who are not players position themselves to support the goal of the team. Each player and team member has a different specialization that contributes to the whole. The team matures over time taking into account feedback from experience, best practice and current processes and procedures to become an agile high-performing team.

Specialization allows for expert focus on components of the service but components of the service also need to work together for value. Coordination across the lifecycle creates an environment focused on business and customer outcomes instead of just IT objectives and projects. Specialization combined with coordination helps to manage expertise, improve focus and reduce overlaps and gaps in processes.

Adopting technology to automate the processes and provide management information that supports the processes is also important for effective and efficient service management.

2.4.2   Processes through the service lifecycle

Each core ITIL publication includes guidance on service management processes as shown in Table 2.1.

Table 2.1 The processes described in each core ITIL publication

Core ITIL lifecycle publication	Processes described in the publication
ITIL Service Strategy	Strategy management for IT services Service portfolio management Financial management for IT services Demand management Business relationship management
ITIL Service Design	Design coordination Service catalogue management Service level management Availability management Capacity management IT service continuity management Information security management Supplier management

Table continues

Table 2.1 *continued*

Core ITIL lifecycle publication	Processes described in the publication
ITIL Service Transition	Transition planning and support Change management Service asset and configuration management Release and deployment management Service validation and testing Change evaluation Knowledge management
ITIL Service Operation	Event management Incident management Request fulfilment Problem management Access management
ITIL Continual Service Improvement	Seven-step improvement process

Most ITIL roles, processes and functions have activities that take place across multiple stages of the service lifecycle. For example:

■ Service validation and testing may design tests during the service design stage and perform these tests during service transition.
■ Technical management provides input to strategic decisions about technology, and assists in the design and transition of infrastructure.

- Business relationship managers assist in gathering requirements during the service design stage of the lifecycle, and take part in the management of major incidents during the service operation stage.

The strength of the service lifecycle relies on continual feedback throughout each stage of the lifecycle. At every point in the service lifecycle, monitoring, assessment and feedback drives decisions about the need for minor course corrections or major service improvement initiatives.

3 Continual service improvement principles

Continual service improvement (CSI) is concerned with identifying ways in which services (and elements of services, such as processes and people) can improve in quality or reduce costs or both. Therefore, CSI must focus on increasing the efficiency, maximizing the effectiveness and optimizing the cost of services and the underlying IT service management (ITSM) processes. The only way to do this is to ensure that improvement opportunities are identified throughout the entire service lifecycle.

3.1 CONTINUAL SERVICE IMPROVEMENT APPROACH

Figure 3.1 shows an overall approach to CSI and illustrates a continual cycle of improvement. This approach to improvement can be summarized as follows:

- Embrace the vision by understanding the high-level business objectives. The vision should align the business and IT strategies.
- Assess the situation to analyse the current position in terms of the business, organization, people, process, technology and suppliers.
- Understand and agree on the priorities for improvement based on a deeper development of the principles defined in the vision.
- Detail the CSI plan to achieve higher-quality service provision by implementing or improving ITSM services.
- Verify that measurements and metrics are in place and that the milestones and the business objectives have been achieved.

Finally, the approach should ensure that the momentum for quality improvement is maintained by assuring that changes become embedded in the organization.

Figure 3.1 Continual service improvement approach

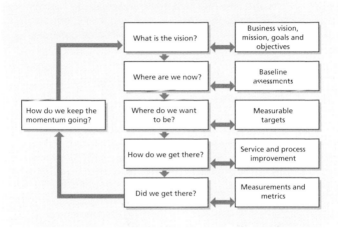

3.2   RETURN ON INVESTMENT AND ESTABLISHING THE BUSINESS CASE

For all improvement opportunities there is a need to understand the return on investment (ROI) or value on investment (VOI) if there is no financial return. On one side, ROI is the investment cost – this is the money an organization pays to improve services and service management processes. On the other side, it is what an organization can gain in return.

The business case should articulate the reason for undertaking a service or process improvement initiative. As far as possible, data and evidence should be provided relating to the costs and expected benefits of undertaking the improvement.

In developing a business case, the focus should not be limited to ROI but should also consider VOI, the business value that service improvement brings to the organization and its customers, because ROI alone does not capture the real value of service improvement.

3.3   CSI AND ORGANIZATIONAL CHANGE

Improving service management often means that at least an element of organizational change is required. Many organizational change programmes fail to achieve the desired results. Successful ITSM requires an understanding of the way in which work is done, and putting in place a programme of change within the IT organization. This type of change is, by its very nature, prone to difficulties. It involves people and the way they work. People generally do not like to change; the benefits must be explained to everyone to gain their support and to ensure that they break out of old working practices. Section 6.4 discusses organizational change in more detail.

3.4   OWNERSHIP

The principle of ownership is fundamental to any improvement strategy. CSI is a best practice, and one of the keys to successful implementation is to ensure that a specific manager, a CSI manager, is accountable for ensuring that best practice is adopted and sustained throughout the organization. The CSI manager is accountable for the success of CSI in the organization, although many others will be responsible for implementing improvement initiatives.

3.5   CSI REGISTER

The CSI register is a single repository where all ideas, initiatives and possibilities for improvement are recorded. All entries should be categorized into small, medium or large undertakings and sub-categorized into quick, medium- and longer-term pieces of work. Each initiative should also show the business outcomes and benefits that will be achieved by its implementation. With all this information it will be possible to prioritize the entries in the register. The CSI register will therefore provide a coordinated, consistent view of the potentially many improvement activities.

3.6   EXTERNAL AND INTERNAL DRIVERS

There are two major areas within every organization driving improvement: aspects that are external to the organization (such as regulation, legislation, competition, external customer requirements, market pressures and economics) and aspects that are internal to the organization (such as organizational structures, culture, new knowledge, new technologies, new skills, existing and projected staffing levels, union rules etc.).

3.7   ASSESSMENTS

A formal assessment is an ideal way of identifying improvement requirements. The value and the maturity of the processes in particular can be assessed. Benchmarking is a specific type of assessment for evaluating various aspects of an organization's services and processes in relation to best practice, usually within its own sector.

Another type of assessment is a SWOT analysis (examining strengths, weaknesses, opportunities and threats). SWOT is helpful in illuminating significant opportunities for improvement. The strengths and weaknesses focus on the internal aspects of the organization, while opportunities and threats concentrate on aspects external to the organization.

This technique involves the review and analysis of four specific areas of an organization: the internal strengths and weaknesses, and the external opportunities and threats. Once analysed, actions should be taken to:

- Develop, exploit and capitalize on the organization's **strengths**
- Reduce, minimize or remove **weaknesses**
- Take maximum advantage of **opportunities**
- Manage, mitigate and eliminate **threats.**

For all sizes of businesses, private and public organizations, educational institutions, consumers and the individuals working within these organizations, IT services have become an integral means for conducting business. Without IT services many organizations would not be able to deliver the products and services in today's market. As reliance on these IT services increases, so do the expectations for availability, reliability and stability. This is why integration of the business and IT is so important – no longer can they be thought of separately. The same holds true when measuring IT services. It is no longer sufficient to measure and report against the performance of an individual component such as a server or application. IT must now be able to measure and report against an end-to-end service.

3.8 SERVICE LEVEL MANAGEMENT AND KNOWLEDGE MANAGEMENT

The service level management (SLM) and knowledge management (KM) processes are vital to the CSI stage of the service lifecycle. A key element of SLM is reviewing service achievement and identifying where improvements are required, feeding them into CSI. Reviewing achievement will be conducted in the service review meetings and by the continuous monitoring of service targets. The definition of success in IT is the achievement of both the agreed service level and the resulting business outcomes.

Within each service lifecycle stage, data should be captured to enable knowledge gain and an understanding of what is actually happening, thus enabling informed decisions to be made. This is often referred to as the Data-to-Information-to-Knowledge-to-Wisdom (DIKW) structure. All too often an organization will capture the appropriate data but fail to provide a context for the data. Data is a set of discrete facts. Information comes from providing a context for the data. Knowledge is composed of the tacit experiences, ideas, insights, values and judgement of individuals and puts the information into an easy-to-use form which can facilitate decision-making. Wisdom makes use of knowledge to create value through correct and well-informed decisions. Wisdom will lead to better decisions on improvement. Knowledge management is a mainstay of any improvement process.

3.9 THE DEMING CYCLE

W. Edwards Deming proposed the Deming Cycle (or Circle) for quality improvement. This cycle is particularly applicable in CSI. Our goal in using the Deming Cycle (or the PDCA cycle, as it is now more commonly known) is steady, ongoing improvement. It is a fundamental tenet of CSI.

The PDCA cycle is critical at two points in CSI: for implementation of CSI, and for the application of CSI to services and service management processes. At implementation, all four stages of the PDCA cycle are used. With ongoing improvement, CSI draws on the 'check' and 'act' stages to monitor, measure, review and implement initiatives.

The seven-step improvement process fully described in Chapter 4 can be viewed as an example of an implementation of the PDCA cycle, with each of the steps falling within one of the phases of the cycle: Plan, Do, Check, Act.

The PDCA cycle provides steady, ongoing improvement.

3.10 SERVICE MEASUREMENT

There are four reasons to monitor and measure:

- **Validate** Monitoring and measuring to validate previous decisions.
- **Direct** Monitoring and measuring to set the direction for activities in order to meet set targets; this is the most prevalent reason for monitoring and measuring.
- **Justify** Monitoring and measuring to justify, with factual evidence or proof, that a course of action is required.

■ **Intervene** Monitoring and measuring to identify a point of intervention, including subsequent changes and corrective actions.

The four basic reasons to monitor and measure lead to three key questions: 'Why are we monitoring and measuring?', 'When do we stop?' and 'Is anyone using the data?'

There are three types of metrics that an organization will need to collect to support CSI activities:

■ **Technology metrics** Typically components and application-based.
■ **Process metrics** Captured in the form of critical success factors (CSFs), key performance indicators (KPIs) and activity metrics for the service management processes. Process metrics can help to determine the overall health of a process. KPIs can help to answer key questions on quality, performance, value and compliance in following the process. CSI would use these metrics as input in identifying improvement opportunities for each process.
■ **Service metrics** A measure of the end-to-end service performance.

3.11 FRAMEWORKS, MODELS, STANDARDS AND QUALITY SYSTEMS

At least to some extent, all governance or quality frameworks and standards have an element of continual improvement embedded within them. As well as ITIL itself these include:

■ Quality management system ISO 9000
■ Total Quality Management (TQM)
■ Management of Risk (M_o_R)

- Control OBjectives for Information and related Technology (COBIT)
- ISO/IEC 20000 and other ISO standards for IT
- ISO 14001 – Environmental management standard
- Programme and project management including PRINCE2
- Skills Framework for the Information Age (SFIA)
- Capability Maturity Model Integration (CMMI)
- ISO/IEC 27001 – Information security management system.

(See Chapter 9 for further information on related guidance.)

Experience has shown that while each may be complete in itself, none provides a total answer for IT management. Indeed, there is a good deal of overlap between these frameworks and standards but, for the most part, they are not competitive or exclusive but complementary. In fact, many organizations use a combination to improve and manage IT more effectively.

An effective CSI practice will be integrated within all stages of the service lifecycle. The greatest value to the business and IT will be realized by having a continuous monitoring and feedback loop as the service and ITSM processes move through the service lifecycle. Look for improvement opportunities within service strategy, service design, service transition and service operation. It is imperative that the concept of continual improvement be woven into the day-to-day fabric of the organization.

3.12   CSI INPUTS AND OUTPUTS

CSI takes input from all stages of the lifecycle including the vision and strategy from service strategy, the service catalogue and all elements of design from service design, test reports from service transition, and achievements against metrics, KPIs and CSFs from service operation. CSI will also produce output for all lifecycle stages such as process improvement ideas.

4 Continual service improvement processes

4.1 THE SEVEN-STEP IMPROVEMENT PROCESS

The seven-step improvement process is concerned with identifying improvement opportunities by measuring and analysing relevant data. Figure 4.1 shows the interaction between the seven-step improvement process and the Plan-Do-Check-Act (PDCA) cycle.

Figure 4.1 also shows how the cycle fits into the Data-to-Information-to-Knowledge-to-Wisdom (DIKW) structure of knowledge management. The integration of the PDCA cycle and the seven-step improvement process is as follows:

- Plan
  1. Identify the strategy for improvement
  2. Define what you will measure
- Do
  3. Gather the data
  4. Process the data
- Check
  5. Analyse the information and data
  6. Present and use the information
- Act
  7. Implement improvement.

Figure 4.1 The seven-step improvement process

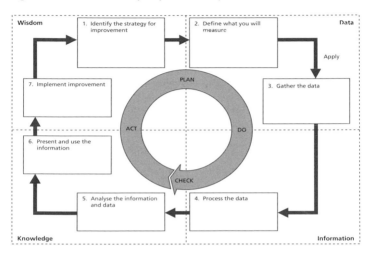

4.1.1 Purpose and objectives

The purpose of the seven-step improvement process is to define and manage the steps needed to identify, define, gather, process, analyse, present and implement improvements.

The objectives of the seven-step improvement process are to:

■ Identify opportunities for improving services, processes, tools etc.

- Reduce the cost of providing services and ensuring that IT services enable the required business outcomes to be achieved. Cost reduction will not result in all cases, as improvement in quality may be the objective.
- Identify what needs to be measured, analysed and reported to establish improvement opportunities.
- Continually review service achievements to ensure that they remain matched to business requirements; continually align and re-align service provision with outcome requirements.

4.1.2   Scope

The seven-step improvement process includes analysis of the performance and capabilities of services and processes throughout the lifecycle. It includes the continual alignment of the portfolio of IT services with the current and future business needs as well as the maturity of the enabling IT processes for each service. It also includes making best use of the technology that the organization has, and looks to exploit new technology as it becomes available where there is a business case for doing so. Also within the scope are the organizational structure; the capabilities of the personnel; and asking whether people are working in appropriate functions and roles, and if they have the required skills.

4.1.3   Value to business

The value of the seven-step improvement process is that by monitoring and analysing the delivery of services, it will ensure that the current and future business outcome requirements can be met. The seven-step improvement process enables continual assessment of the current situation against business needs, and identifies opportunities to improve service provision for customers.

4.1.4 Policies, principles and basic concepts

The seven-step improvement process puts a structure in place to enable continual assessment of the current situation against business needs, and looks for opportunities to improve service provision, thus enabling the overall business to be more successful.

4.1.4.1 Policies

Many of the policies that support the seven-step improvement process are often found as parts of other processes. Examples of some of these policies are:

- Monitoring requirements must be defined and implemented.
- Data must be gathered and analysed and its integrity checked on a consistent basis.
- Trend reporting must be provided on a consistent basis.
- Service level achievement reports must be provided on a consistent basis.
- Internal and external service reviews must be completed on a consistent basis ('internal' here means within IT and 'external' with the business).
- Services must have either clearly defined service levels or service targets that can be used to determine whether there are gaps in the services provided.

- Service management processes must have critical success factors (CSFs) and key performance indicators (KPIs) to determine whether there are gaps between the expected outcome and the actual outcome.
- All improvement initiatives must use the formal change management process.
- All functional groups within IT have a responsibility for CSI activities. This might be only one person in the group, but the intent here is that CSI is not usually a functional group within an organization but that everyone has a hand in supporting CSI activities.

4.1.4.2   Principles

Many service providers operate in a competitive environment and they need to continually assess their services against market expectations to ensure that they remain competitive. Also, new delivery mechanisms (e.g. cloud computing) can introduce service efficiencies and need to be reviewed. The following activities should be regularly performed:

- Services must be checked against competitive service offerings to ensure that they continue to add true business value to the client, and that the service provider remains competitive in its delivery of such services.
- Services must be reviewed in the light of new technological advances to ensure that they are delivering the most efficient services to the customer.

4.1.4.3   Basic concepts

CSI is often viewed as an ad hoc activity within IT services; the activity is only triggered when someone in IT management flags up that there is a problem. This is not the right way to address CSI. Often, these reactive events are not even providing continual improvement, but simply stopping a single failure from occurring again.

CSI needs a commitment from everyone in IT working throughout the service lifecycle to be successful at improving services and service management processes. It requires ongoing attention, a well-thought-out plan, and consistent attention to monitoring, analysing and reporting results with an eye towards improvement.

IT services must ensure that appropriate resources and tools are identified and implemented to support CSI activities. It is also important to understand the difference between what *should* be measured and what *can* be measured. Start small – don't expect to measure everything at once. Understand the organizational capability to gather and process the data. Be sure to spend time analysing data as this is where the real value comes in.

An organization can find improvement opportunities throughout the entire service lifecycle. An IT organization does not need to wait until a service or service management process is transitioned into the operations area to begin identifying improvement opportunities.

4.1.5 Process activities, methods and techniques

The seven-step improvement process is shown in Figure 4.1. Figure 4.2 illustrates the trail from vision to measurements. Elements from this trail are used at points throughout the seven-step improvement process, and each step is described in further detail below.

Figure 4.2 From vision to measurements

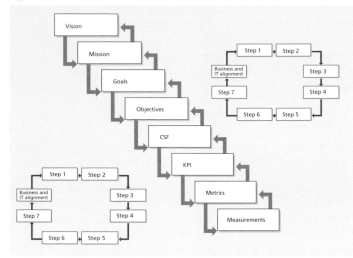

4.1.5.1   Step 1 – Identify the strategy for improvement

Before any further activity can be started, it is imperative that the overall vision is identified. What are we trying to achieve for the business as a whole? The questions we need to ask are: What initiatives does the business have that could be undermined by poor IT service provision? Or, more positively: How can improvements in IT enable the business vision to be achieved? The answers to these questions will come from working through the seven-step improvement process.

Like all the steps in the process, this first stage should be revisited to reassess the potentially changing vision and goals. When reconsidering this process we would apply any wisdom gained from previous iterations.

Inputs for this step are:

- Business plans and strategy
- Service review meetings
- Customer satisfaction surveys
- Vision and mission statements
- Corporate, divisional and departmental goals and objectives
- Legislative requirements
- Governance requirements
- CSI initiatives as logged in the CSI register.

4.1.5.2 Step 2 – Define what you will measure

This step is directly related to the strategic, tactical and operational goals that have been defined for measuring services and service management processes as well as the existing technology and capability to support measuring and CSI activities. In this step you need to define what you should measure; define what you can actually measure; carry out a gap analysis; and then finalize the actual measurement plan.

Measurement will take place at service, process and technology levels.

Step 2 is iterative during the rest of the activities.

Compile a list of what you should measure driven by business requirements. Do not try to cover every single eventuality or possible metric; make it simple. The number of items you should measure can grow rapidly. So too can the number of metrics and measurements.

The following are some other potential areas for measurement:

- **Service levels** As well as normal SLA targets you may need to collect availability management measures such as mean time to repair (MTTR) and mean time to restore service (MTRS).
- **Customer satisfaction** Surveys are conducted on a continual basis to measure and track how satisfied customers are with the IT organization.
- **Business impact** Measure what actions are invoked for any disruption in service that adversely affects the customer's business operation, processes or its own customers.
- **Supplier performance** Whenever an organization has entered into a supplier relationship where some services or parts of services have been outsourced or co-sourced, it is important to measure the performance of the supplier.
- **Market performance** This ensures that the services remain aligned with those being delivered by other service providers in the IT service delivery community.

One of CSI's key sets of activities is to measure, analyse and report on IT services and IT service management (ITSM) results. Measurements produce data, which should be analysed over time to produce a trend. This will tell a story that may be good or bad. It is essential that measurements of this kind have ongoing relevance. What was important to know last year may no longer be pertinent this year.

4.1.5.3 Step 3 – Gather the data

Gathering data requires monitoring to be in place. Monitoring could be executed using technology such as application-, system- and component-monitoring tools as used in the event management process (documented in *ITIL Service Operation*) or it could even be a manual process for certain tasks. The accuracy and integrity of the data should always be maintained.

Quality is the key objective of monitoring for CSI. Monitoring will therefore focus on the effectiveness and efficiency of a service, process, tool, organization or configuration item (CI). The emphasis is not on assuring real-time service performance; rather it is on identifying where improvements can be made to the existing level of service, or IT performance. Monitoring for CSI will therefore tend to focus on detecting exceptions and resolutions. For example, CSI is not simply interested in whether an incident was resolved, but whether it was resolved within the agreed time, and whether future incidents can be prevented.

Each organization will need to collect technology, process and service metrics, as described in section 3.10.

Service management monitoring helps to determine the health and welfare of service management processes in the following manner:

- **Process compliance** Are the processes being followed?
- **Quality** How well are the processes working? Monitor the individual or key activities as they relate to the objectives of the end-to-end process.
- **Performance** How fast or slow is the process? Monitor efficiency – e.g. throughput or cycle times.

■ **Value** Is this making a difference? Monitor the effectiveness and perceived value of the process to the stakeholders and the IT staff executing the process activities.

■ **Volume** Determine the loading and throughput on the service management processes (e.g. number of incidents or number of changes).

Monitoring should also be used for checking staff behaviour such as adherence to process activities and use of authorized tools, as well as project schedules and budgets.

Inputs to gathering the data include:

■ New business requirements
■ Existing SLAs
■ Existing monitoring and data capture capability
■ Plans from other processes, e.g. availability management and capacity management
■ The CSI register and existing service improvement plans (SIPs)
■ Previous trend analysis reports
■ List of what you *should* measure
■ List of what you *can* measure
■ Gap analysis report
■ List of what to measure
■ Customer satisfaction surveys.

4.1.5.4   Step 4 – Process the data

In this step the data is converted into the required format for the required audience. Follow the trail from metrics to KPI to CSF, all the way back to the vision if necessary.

Report-generating technologies are typically used at this stage as various amounts of data are condensed into information for use in the analysis activity. The data is also usually put into a format that provides an end-to-end perspective on the overall performance of a service. This activity begins with the transformation of raw data into packaged information. Use the information to develop insight into the performance of the service and/or processes. Process the data into information (by creating logical groupings), which provides a better means to analyse the information and data – the next step in the seven-step process.

The output of logical groupings could be contained in spreadsheets, reports generated directly from the service management tool suite, system monitoring and reporting tools.

Examples of outputs of processing data from procedures include:

- Updated availability and capacity plans
- Reports
- Logical groupings of data ready for analysis.

4.1.5.5   Step 5 – Analyse the information and data

If your organization's service desk has a trend of reduced call volumes consistently over the last four months, you need to ask yourself the question: 'Is this a good trend or a bad trend?' You don't know whether the call reduction is because you have reduced the number of recurring errors in the infrastructure by good problem management activities; it might be that the customers feel that the service desk doesn't provide any value and have started bypassing the service desk, going directly to second-level support groups.

Data analysis transforms the information into knowledge of events that are affecting the organization. More skill and experience is required to perform data analysis than data gathering and processing. Verification against goals and objectives is expected during this activity. This verification validates that objectives are being supported and value is being added. It is not sufficient simply to produce graphs of various types – the observations and conclusions must be documented.

4.1.5.6   Step 6 – Present and use the information

The sixth step is to take our knowledge, which is represented in the reports, monitors, action plans, reviews, evaluations and opportunities, and present it to the target audience in a clear, digestible and timely way. This step is synonymous with service reporting. Consider the target audience; make sure that you identify the exceptions to the service, and the benefits that have been revealed, or can be expected. Data gathering occurs at the operational level of an organization. In the sixth step this data needs to be formatted to enable insight into needs and expectations.

This stage involves presenting the information in a format that is understandable, at the right level, provides value, notes exceptions to service, identifies benefits that were revealed during the time period, and allows those receiving the information to make strategic, tactical and operational decisions.

CSI is an ongoing activity of monitoring and gathering data, processing the data into logical groupings, and analysing it in order to meet targets and identify trends and improvement opportunities. There is no value in all the work done to this point if we don't do a good job of presenting our findings and then using them to make decisions that will lead to improvements.

There are usually four distinct audiences:

- **Customers** Their real need is to understand whether IT delivered the service at the promised levels and, if not, what improvements are being implemented to rectify the situation.
- **Senior IT management** This group is often focused on the results surrounding CSFs and KPIs, such as customer satisfaction, actual versus plan, and costing and revenue targets. Information provided at this level helps determine strategic and tactical improvements on a larger scale.
- **Internal IT** This group is often interested in KPIs and activity metrics that help them plan, coordinate, schedule and identify incremental improvement opportunities.
- **Suppliers** This group will be interested in KPIs and activity metrics related to their own services and performance. Suppliers may also be targeted with improvement initiatives.

Often there is a gap between what the IT service provider reports and what is of interest to the business. IT might report on an element of the service such as server availability rather than the end-to-end service. What the business wants to understand is the number of outages that occurred and the duration of the outages, with an analysis describing the impact on the business processes: in essence, unavailability expressed in a commonly understood measure – time. Of course, what the business is really interested in is what the service provider is going to do to prevent it happening again.

4.1.5.7 Step 7 – Implement improvement

Use the knowledge gained and combine it with previous experience to make informed decisions about optimizing, improving and correcting services. Managers need to identify issues and present solutions.

This stage may include any number of activities, such as approval of improvement activities, prioritization and submitting a business case, integration with change management, integration with other lifecycle stages, guidance on how to manage an ongoing improvement project successfully, and checking whether the improvement actually achieved its objective.

CSI may identify many opportunities for improvement, but organizations cannot afford to implement all of them. An organization needs to prioritize improvement activities for its goals, objectives, return on investment (ROI), types of service breaches etc., and document them in the CSI register. Improvement initiatives can also be externally driven by regulatory requirements, changes in competition, or even political decisions.

Inputs include:

- Knowledge gained from presenting and using the information
- Agreed implementation plans (from Step 6)
- A CSI register for those initiatives that have been started from other sources such as assessments.

4.1.6   Triggers, inputs, outputs and interfaces

4.1.6.1   Triggers, inputs and outputs

Monitoring to identify improvement opportunities is and must be an ongoing process. New improvement incentives may trigger additional measurement activity.

Many inputs and outputs to the process are documented within the steps, but examples of key inputs include:

- Service catalogue
- Service level requirements (SLRs)
- The service review meeting
- Vision and mission statements
- Corporate, divisional and departmental goals and objectives
- Legislative requirements
- Governance requirements
- Budget cycle
- Customer satisfaction surveys
- The overall IT strategy
- Market expectations (especially in relation to competitive IT service providers)
- New technology drivers (e.g. cloud-based delivery and external hosting)
- Flexible commercial models (e.g. low capital expenditure and high operational expenditure commercial models, and rental models).

4.1.6.2   Interfaces

In order to support improvement activities it is important to have the CSI seven-step improvement process integrated within each service lifecycle stage including the underlying processes residing in each lifecycle stage. Each step of the CSI lifecycle will be involved in every one of the other lifecycle stages.

Examples include monitoring the progress of strategies, standards, policies and architectural decisions that have been made and implemented. Service strategy will also analyse results associated with implemented strategies, policies and standards.

Within the service design stage, monitoring and gathering data are associated with creating and modifying services and service management processes. This part of the service lifecycle also measures against the effectiveness and ability to measure CSFs and KPIs that were defined through gathering business requirements. It is during service design that the definition of what should be measured is produced.

Service transition develops and tests the monitoring procedures and criteria to be used during and after implementation. Service transition monitors and gathers data on the actual release into production of services and service management processes. Service transition develops the monitoring procedures and criteria to be used during and after implementation.

It is during the service operation lifecycle stage that the actual monitoring of services in the live environment takes place. People working in the service operation functions will play a large part in the processing activity.

The seven-step improvement process receives and collects the data as an input. If there is a CSI functional group within an organization, it can be the single point for combining all analysis, trend data and comparison of results to targets. This group could then review all proposed improvement opportunities, help to prioritize the opportunities and finally make a consolidated recommendation to senior management. For smaller organizations, this may fall to an individual or smaller group acting as a coordinating point and owning CSI. This is a key point. Too often data is gathered in the various technical domains never to be heard of again. Designating a CSI group provides a single place in the organization for all the data to reside and be analysed.

All the ITIL processes have responsibility for continual improvement of the process itself. The process metrics will indicate where improvements or cost reductions can be made. Some of the key processes related to general improvement are documented below.

4.1.7 Critical success factors and key performance indicators

Examples of CSFs and KPIs for seven-step improvement include:

- **CSF** All improvement opportunities identified
  - **KPI** Percentage improvement in defects; for example, 3% reduction in failed changes; 10% reduction in security breaches
- **CSF** The cost of providing services is reduced
  - **KPI** Percentage decrease in overall cost of service provision; for example, 2.5% reduction in the average cost of handling an incident; 5% reduction in the cost of processing a particular type of transaction
- **CSF** The required business outcomes from IT services are achieved
  - **KPI** For instance, a 3% increase in customer satisfaction with the service desk; 2% increase in customer satisfaction with the warranty offered by the payroll service.

4.1.8   Challenges and risks

Challenges facing organizations when implementing CSI include:

- Getting the required resources to implement and run the process
- Gathering the right level of data
- Having the tools to manipulate the data
- Encouraging the IT organization to approach CSI in a consistent and structured way
- Making IT managers realize that there is another way, and getting commitment from management to approach it in that better way
- Obtaining sufficient information from the business regarding improvement requirements and cost reductions
- Persuading suppliers to include improvement in their contractual agreements; this is especially relevant for outsourced services.

There are several risks that could prevent CSI from achieving the overall desired effect:

- No formalized approach to CSI, and initiatives being taken on randomly in an ad hoc manner
- Insufficient monitoring and analysis to identify the areas of greatest need
- Staff attitudes such as 'We have always done it this way and it has always been good enough'
- Inability to make the business case for improvement and therefore no funding for improvement initiatives
- Lack of ownership or loss of ownership
- Too much focus on IT improvements without a clear understanding of business needs and objectives.

5 Organizing for continual service improvement

There is no single best way to organize, and best practices described in ITIL need to be tailored to suit each situation, taking into account resource constraints and the size, nature and needs of the business and customers. The starting point for organizational design is service strategy.

Section 2.2.3 of this publication provides an overview of functions and roles.

5.1 FUNCTIONS

For continual service improvement to be successful, an organization will need to define the roles and responsibilities required to undertake the processes and activities identified in this key element guide. These roles should be assigned to individuals, and an appropriate organization structure of teams, groups or functions established and managed.

Continual service improvement does not define specific functions, but it does rely on the technical and application management functions described in *ITIL Service Operation*. Technical and application management provide resources and expertise to manage the whole service lifecycle, and roles within continual service improvement may be performed by members of these functions.

5.2   ROLES

A number of roles need to be performed in support of CSI. The core ITIL publications provide guidelines and examples of role descriptions. In many cases roles will need to be combined or separated depending on the organizational context and size.

A RACI model can be used to define the roles and responsibilities in relation to processes and activities.

RACI is an acronym for:

- **Responsible** The person or people responsible for correct execution – for getting the job done.
- **Accountable** The person who has ownership of quality and the end result.
- **Consulted** The people who are consulted and whose opinions are sought. They have involvement through input of knowledge and information.
- **Informed** The people who are kept up to date on progress. They receive information about process execution and quality.

Only one person should be accountable for any process or individual activity, although several people may be responsible for executing parts of the activity.

Roles fall into two main categories – generic roles such as process manager and process owner, and specific roles that are involved within a particular lifecycle stage or process such as a change administrator or knowledge management process owner.

5.2.1   Generic service owner role

The service owner is accountable for the delivery of a specific IT service and is responsible for the initiation, transition, maintenance and support of that service.

The service owner's responsibilities include:

- Working with business relationship management to ensure that the service provider can meet customer requirements
- Participating in negotiating service level agreements (SLAs) and operational level agreements (OLAs) relating to the service
- Ensuring that ongoing service delivery and support meet agreed customer requirements
- Ensuring consistent and appropriate communication with customer(s) for service-related enquiries and issues
- Representing the service across the organization, including at change advisory board (CAB) meetings
- Serving as the point of escalation (notification) for major incidents relating to the service
- Participating in internal and external service review meetings.

The service owner is responsible for continual improvement and the management of change affecting the service under their care.

5.2.2   Generic process owner role

The process owner role is accountable for ensuring that a process is fit for purpose, is performed according to agreed standards and meets the aims of the process definition. This role is often assigned to the same person who carries out the process manager role, but the two roles may be separate in larger organizations.

The process owner's accountabilities include:

■ Sponsoring, designing and change managing the process and its metrics

■ Defining appropriate policies and standards for the process, with periodic auditing to ensure compliance

■ Providing process resources to support activities required throughout the service lifecycle

■ Ensuring that process technicians understand their role and have the required knowledge to deliver the process

■ Addressing issues with running the process

■ Identifying enhancement and improvement opportunities and making improvements to the process.

5.2.3   Generic process manager role

The process manager role is accountable for operational management of a process. There may be several process managers for one process, for example covering different locations.

The process manager's accountabilities include:

■ Working with the process owner to plan and coordinate all process activities

■ Ensuring that all activities are carried out as required throughout the service lifecycle

■ Appointing people to the required roles and managing assigned resources

■ Monitoring and reporting on process performance

■ Identifying opportunities for and making improvements to the process.

5.2.4   Generic process practitioner role

The process practitioner's responsibilities include:

- Carrying out one or more activities of a process
- Understanding how their role contributes to the overall delivery of service and creation of value for the business
- Ensuring that inputs, outputs and interfaces for their activities are correct
- Creating or updating records to show that activities have been carried out correctly.

5.2.5   CSI manager

The role of CSI manager is essential for a successful improvement programme. The CSI manager is ultimately responsible for the success of all improvement activities. This single point of accountability, coupled with competence and authority, improves the chances of a successful improvement programme. A single person can fulfil the role of the CSI manager and the role of the seven-step improvement process owner or manager.

The CSI manager's responsibilities typically include:

- Developing the CSI domain
- Communicating the vision of CSI across the IT organization
- Ensuring that CSI roles have been filled
- Designing the CSI register and associated activities
- Working with service owners, service level managers, the seven-step improvement process manager and other process managers and functions to identify, prioritize and manage improvement opportunities for inclusion in the CSI register
- Working with service level managers to ensure that monitoring requirements are defined

- Ensuring that baseline data is captured to measure improvement against it
- Defining and creating reports on CSI critical success factors (CSFs), key performance indicators (KPIs) and CSI activity metrics
- Identifying other frameworks, models and standards that will support CSI activities
- Ensuring that CSI activities are coordinated throughout the service lifecycle
- Presenting recommendations for improvement to senior management
- Building effective relationships with the business and IT senior managers
- Identifying and delivering process improvements in critical business areas across manufacturing and relevant divisions
- Setting direction and providing a framework through which improvement objectives can be delivered
- Coaching, mentoring and supporting fellow service improvement professionals.

The CSI manager should possess the ability to influence positively all levels of management, to ensure that service improvement activities are receiving the necessary support and are resourced sufficiently to implement solutions.

5.2.6 Seven-step improvement roles

This section describes a number of roles that need to be performed in support of the seven-step improvement process.

5.2.6.1 Seven-step improvement process owner

The seven-step improvement process owner's responsibilities typically include:

- Carrying out the generic process owner role for the seven-step improvement process
- Working with the CSI manager, service owners, process owners and functions to include appropriate elements of the seven-step improvement process throughout the service lifecycle.

5.2.6.2 Seven-step improvement process manager

The seven-step improvement process manager's responsibilities typically include:

- Carrying out the generic process manager role for the seven-step improvement process
- Planning and managing support for improvement tools and processes
- Working with the CSI manager, service owners, process owners and functions to maintain the CSI register
- Coordinating interfaces between the seven-step improvement process, other processes, service managers and functions.

5.2.6.3 Reporting analyst

The reporting analyst is a key role for CSI and will often work closely with SLM. The reporting analyst reviews and analyses data from components, systems and sub-systems in order to obtain a true end-to-end service achievement. The reporting analyst will also identify trends and establish if they are positive or negative. This information is then used to present the data.

The reporting analyst's responsibilities typically include:

■ Participating in CSI meetings and SLM meetings to ensure the validity of the reporting metrics, notification thresholds and overall solution
■ Consolidating data from multiple sources
■ Producing trends and providing feedback on the trends such as whether the trends are positive or negative, what their impact is likely to be, and if they are predictable for the future
■ Producing reports on service or system performance based on the negotiated OLAs and SLAs and improvement initiatives.

The reporting analyst's key skills and competencies typically include:

■ Good understanding of statistical and analytical principles and processes
■ Strong technical foundation in the reporting tool(s)
■ Good communication skills
■ Good technical understanding and an ability to translate technical requirements and specifications into easily understood reporting requirements.

5.2.6.4 Other roles involved in the seven-step improvement process

In addition to the specific roles and activities described above, many activities of the seven-step improvement process take place in other processes and functions throughout the service lifecycle. CSI will only be successful if the required activities are clearly identified and assigned to appropriate roles.

Figure 5.1 lists the nature of many of these activities and the skills required to perform them.

Figure 5.1 Activities and skill levels needed for continual service improvement

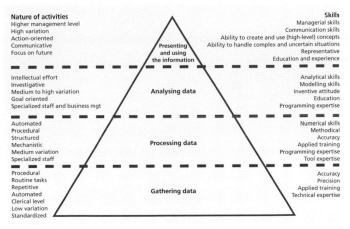

Nature of activities

Presenting and using the information
Higher management level
High variation
Action-oriented
Communicative
Focus on future

Analysing data
Intellectual effort
Investigative
Medium to high variation
Goal oriented
Specialized staff and business mgt

Processing data
Automated
Procedural
Structured
Mechanistic
Medium variation
Specialized staff

Gathering data
Procedural
Routine tasks
Repetitive
Automated
Clerical level
Low variation
Standardized

Skills

Presenting and using the information:
Managerial skills
Communication skills
Ability to create and use (high-level) concepts
Ability to handle complex and uncertain situations
Representative
Education and experience

Analysing data:
Analytical skills
Modelling skills
Inventive attitude
Education
Programming expertise

Processing data:
Numerical skills
Methodical
Accuracy
Applied training
Programming expertise
Tool expertise

Gathering data:
Accuracy
Precision
Applied training
Technical expertise

Note: Figure 5.1 covers steps 3 to 6 of the seven-step improvement process described in Chapter 4. The following section expands on this by detailing each step in the seven-step improvement process and highlighting related activities and skills in each of the seven steps.

Step 1 – Identify the strategy for improvement

Roles: individuals involved with strategic decision-making on the vision for the business and how IT enables that vision to succeed – individuals who will be looking at strategic, technical and operational goals.

Examples: strategy manager, service owner, service level manager, CSI manager, customers, senior business managers, business/IT analysts and senior IT managers (see Table 5.1).

Table 5.1 Skills involved in Step 1 – Identify the strategy for improvement

Nature of activities	Skills
Senior management	Ability to create a high-level vision and strategy
High variation	Communication
Action-oriented	Ability to create and use high-level concepts
Communicative	Ability to handle complex/uncertain situations
Focused on future	Ability to set longer-term goals

Step 2 – Define what you will measure

Roles: individuals involved with decision-making from IT and the business who understand the internal and external factors that influence the necessary elements which should be measured to support the business, governance and, possibly, regulatory legislation; individuals involved with providing the service (internal and external providers) who understand the capabilities of the measuring processes, procedures, tools and staff.

Examples: service owner, service level manager, CSI manager, process owner, process managers, customers, business/IT analysts, senior IT managers, and internal and external providers (see Table 5.2).

Table 5.2 Skills involved in Step 2 – Define what you will measure

Nature of activities	Skills
Senior management	Managerial
High variation	Communication
Action-oriented	Ability to create and use (high-level) concepts
Communicative	Ability to handle complex/uncertain situations
Intellectual effort	Analytical
Investigative	Modelling
Medium to high variation	Inventive attitude

Step 3 – Gather the data

Roles: individuals involved in day-to-day process activities within the lifecycle stages, in particular in the operational aspects of the processes where the results of many of the processes can be collected.

Examples: service desk staff, technical management staff, application management staff, IT security staff and many more (see Table 5.3).

Table 5.3 Skills involved in Step 3 – Gather the data

Nature of activities	Skills
Procedural	Accuracy
Routine	Precision
Repetitive	Meticulous nature
Automated	Technical ability
Clerical	Ability to document

Step 4 – Process the data

Roles: individuals involved in day-to-day process activities within the lifecycle stages.

Examples: service desk staff, technical management staff, application management staff and IT security staff (see Table 5.4).

Table 5.4 Skills involved in Step 4 – Process the data

Nature of activities	Skills
Automated	Numerical
Procedural	Methodical
Structural	Accuracy
Mechanistic	Meticulous nature
Medium variation	Programming skills
Specialized	Tool and technical skills and experience

Step 5 – Analyse the information and data

Roles: individuals involved with providing the service (internal and external providers) who understand the capabilities of the measuring services, processes, procedures, tools and staff.

Examples: service owner, process owner, process managers, business/IT analysts, senior IT analysts, supervisors and team leaders (see Table 5.5).

Table 5.5 Skills involved in Step 5 – Analyse the information and data

Nature of activities	Skills
Intellectual	Analytical
Investigative	Modelling
Medium to high variation	Inventive attitude
Goal-oriented	Ambitious
Specialized and business management	Programming skills

Step 6 – Present and use the information

Roles: individuals involved with providing the service (internal and external providers) who understand the capabilities of the service and the underpinning processes, and who possess good communication skills; key personnel involved with decision-making from IT and the business.

Examples: CSI manager, service owner, service level manager, process owner, process managers, customers, business/IT analysts, senior IT managers, internal and external providers (see Table 5.6).

Table 5.6 Skills involved in Step 6 – Present and use the information

Nature of activities	Skills
Higher management	Managerial
High variation	Communication
Action-oriented	Ability to create, use (high-level) concepts
Communicative	Ability to handle complex/ uncertain situations
Focused on future	Ambitious

Step 7 – Implement improvement

Roles: individuals involved with providing the service (internal and external providers).

Examples: CSI manager, service owner, service level manager, process owner, process managers, customers, business/IT analysts, senior IT managers, and internal and external providers (see Table 5.7).

Table 5.7 Skills involved in Step 7 – Implement improvement

Nature of activities	Skills
Intellectual effort	Analytical
Investigative	Modelling
Medium-to-high variation	Inventive attitude
Goal-oriented	Ambitious
Specialized staff and business management	Programming skills

5.2.7 Business relationship manager

The objective of business relationship management is to establish and maintain a good relationship between the service provider and the customer, based on understanding the customer and their business drivers. The customer's business drivers could require changes in SLAs and thus become input into service improvement opportunities. *ITIL Service Strategy* provides more detail on business relationship management and the role of business relationship managers.

Business relationship managers work closely with service level managers, service owners and the CSI manager to deliver high-quality services. Their roles are compared in Table 5.8.

Table 5.8 Comparison of CSI manager, service level manager, service owner and business relationship manager roles

	CSI manager	Service level manager	Service owner	Business relationship manager
Focus				
IT services	S	P	P	P
IT systems	S		P	
Processes	P	S	S	S
Customers	S	P	S	P
Technology	P	S	P	
Responsibilities				
Developing and maintaining the catalogue of existing services		P	S	P
Developing and maintaining OLAs		P	S	
Gathering service level requirements (SLRs) from the customer	S	P	S	P
Negotiating and maintaining SLAs with the customer	S	P	S	S
Understanding underpinning contracts (UCs) as they relate to OLAs and SLAs	S	P	S	S
Ensuring that appropriate service level monitoring is in place	P	P	S	

	CSI manager	Service level manager	Service owner	Business relationship manager
Responsibilities *continued*				
Producing, reviewing and evaluating reports on service performance and achievements regularly	P	P	P	P
Conducting regular meetings with the customer to discuss service level performance and improvement	S	P	S	S
Conducting yearly SLA review meetings with the customer	S	P	S	S
Ensuring customer satisfaction with the use of a customer satisfaction survey	S	P	S	P
Initiating appropriate actions to improve service levels through service improvement plans (SIPs)	P	P	P	P
Negotiating and agreeing OLAs and SLAs	S	P	S	S
Ensuring the management of UCs as they relate to OLAs and SLAs	S	S	S	
Working with the service level manager to provide services to meet the customer's requirements	P		P	P
Appropriate monitoring of services or systems	P	P	S	
Producing, reviewing and evaluating reports on service or system performance and achievement to the service level manager and the service level process manager	P	P	P	S
P = primary responsibility; S = secondary responsibility; Blank = no specific responsibility				

6 Implementing continual service improvement

6.1 CRITICAL CONSIDERATIONS FOR IMPLEMENTING CSI

CSI is implemented from two perspectives: the implementation of CSI activities for services, and the implementation of CSI for service management processes. However, if your organization does not have very mature service management processes then it is usually difficult to execute the seven-step improvement process for services.

Immature processes usually have poor data quality, if any at all. This is often because there are no processes or very ad hoc processes. Other organizations have multiple processes working with multiple tools used to support the processes. If any monitoring is going on, it may be at a component or application level but not from an end-to-end service perspective. In such a situation, there is no central gathering point for data, no resources allocated to process and analyse the data, and reporting consists of too much data broken into too many segments for anyone to analyse. Some organizations don't have any evidence of reporting at all.

Before implementing CSI, it is important to have identified and filled the critical roles. In addition, it will not be possible to make progress with CSI activities until monitoring and reporting on technology metrics, process metrics and service metrics are in place.

Internal service review meetings must be scheduled in order to review from an internal IT perspective the results achieved each month. These internal review meetings should take place before external review meetings with the business.

6.2   WHERE DO I START?

6.2.1   Where do I start – the service approach

An organization can choose to implement CSI activities in many different ways. One method is to identify a certain pain point such as a service that is not consistently achieving the desired results. Work with the service owner to validate the desired results and the trend results over the past few months. Review any monitoring that has been done. If no end-to-end monitoring has been in place but some component monitoring has occurred, then review what has been monitored and see if there are any consistent issues that are leading to the lower than expected service results. Even if no component monitoring has been conducted, review incidents to identify any trends and CIs that are consistently failing more than others that impact the service. Also review the change records for the different CIs that together underpin the service.

The bottom line is that you have to start somewhere. If there is no adequate data from monitoring or from another process, the first step is to identify what to monitor, define the monitoring requirements, and put in place (or begin using) the technology required for monitoring.

Be sure to analyse the data to see if the trends make sense and whether there are any consistent failures or deviations from expected results. Report findings and identify improvement opportunities.

6.2.2   Where do I start – the lifecycle approach

Another approach is to start looking at the output from the different lifecycle stages. For example, service design personnel should monitor and report on their activities, and use trend evaluation and analysis to identify improvement opportunities to implement. This needs to be done at every stage of the service lifecycle, and CSI should be engaged in this activity. Until the service is implemented we may not know if the right strategy was identified, so we may not have any input for service strategy improvement until later.

As service transition personnel begin working with the designed service, they may identify improvement opportunities for service design. CSI can be effective well before a service is implemented into the live environment.

6.2.3   Where do I start – the functional group approach

Perhaps your organization is experiencing a lot of failures or issues with servers. If this is the case, one could argue a good case for focusing CSI activities within the functional group responsible for the servers, as server failures have a direct impact on service availability.

This is only a short-term solution, as CSI activities should be reviewing services from an end-to-end perspective; however, it is often easier to have a small group focused on CSI activities. Perhaps this could be a pilot of CSI activities before a full deployment across the organization.

6.3   GOVERNANCE

Regardless of whether you are implementing CSI for service management or services, it is critical that governance is addressed from a strategic viewpoint. Organizations are facing the need to expand their IT service management strategies from an operational level to tactical and strategic levels in order to address business process automation, market globalization and the increasing dependency on IT for efficient and reliable management and delivery of core business services. Introducing service management processes into internal IT organizations requires a transformation in the IT culture.

Some internal IT organizations are still system/technology-management-based organizations, which are reactive in nature. Changing to a service-management-based organization, which is more proactive in nature, is a step to aligning IT with business. It is also fundamental in achieving the goal of providing efficient and reliable management and delivery of core business services.

Implementing an IT service management (ITSM) process governance organization will support the development of and transformation to a process- and service-based organization and provide the organizational infrastructure to manage improvement initiatives.

6.3.1   Business drivers

The implementation of a standard ITSM framework and governance is deemed imperative to support current and future business plans to:

- Support the organization's vision
- Provide standard IT processes and a stable and reliable IT environment to enable timely and efficient integration of new services and systems

- Provide process policies, standards and controls to comply with internal audit and external regulatory and legislation requirements
- Foster a climate of commitment to best practices
- Provide a standard ITSM framework across the IT organization to support the organizational transformation to an enterprise IT services model, while maintaining operational stability and reliability for the business.

6.4   CSI AND ORGANIZATIONAL CHANGE

Project management structures and frameworks often fail to take into account the softer aspects involved in organizational change, such as overcoming resistance to change, gaining commitment, empowering, motivating, involving and communicating. Experience reveals that it is precisely these aspects that prevent many CSI initiatives from realizing their intended aims. The success of a CSI initiative depends on the buy-in of all stakeholders. Gaining their support from the outset, and keeping it, will ensure their participation in the development process and acceptance of the solution. The first five steps in Table 6.1 identify the basic leadership actions required.

Those responsible for managing and steering the CSI initiative should consciously address these softer issues. Using an approach such as John P. Kotter's 'eight steps to transform your organization', coupled with formalized project management skills and practices, will significantly increase the chance of success.

Kotter, Professor of Leadership at Harvard Business School, investigated more than a hundred companies that were involved in (or had attempted) a complex change programme, and identified eight main steps that need to be implemented in order to successfully change. The eight steps, which are shown in Table 6.1, apply equally to ITSM implementation programmes.

Table 6.1 Eight steps that need to be implemented, and the main reasons why transformation efforts fail (from Kotter, 1996)

Step		Reasons for failure (quotes)
1	Create a sense of urgency	'50% of transformations fail in this phase'
		'Without motivation, people won't help and the effort goes nowhere'
		'76% of a company's management should be convinced of the need'
2	Form a guiding coalition	'Underestimating the difficulties in producing change'
		'Lack of effective, strong leadership'
		'Not a powerful enough guiding coalition … opposition eventually stops the change initiative'
3	Create a vision	'Without a sensible vision, a transformation effort can easily dissolve into a list of confusing, incompatible projects that can take the organization in the wrong direction, or nowhere at all'
		'An explanation of 5 minutes should obtain a reaction of "understanding" and "interest"'

Table continues

Table 6.1 *continued*

4	Communicate the vision	'Without credible communication, and a lot of it, the hearts and minds of the troops are never captured'
		'Make use of all communications channels'
		'Let the managers lead by example ... "walk the talk"'
5	Empower others to act on the vision	'Structures to underpin the vision ... and removal of barriers to change'
		'The more people involved, the better the outcome'
		'Reward initiatives'
6	Plan for and create quick wins	'Real transformation takes time ... without quick wins, too many people give up or join the ranks of those opposing change'
		'Actively look for performance improvements and establish clear goals'
		'Communicate successes'
7	Consolidate improvements and produce more change	'Until changes sink deeply into the culture, new approaches are fragile and subject to regression'
		'In many cases, workers revert to old practice'
		'Use credibility of quick wins to tackle even bigger problems'

Table continues

Table 6.1 *continued*

8	Institutionalize the change	'Show how new approaches, behaviour and attitude have helped improve performance'
		'Ensure selection and promotion criteria underpin the new approach'

6.5   COMMUNICATION STRATEGY AND PLAN

Timely and effective communication forms an important part of any service improvement project. In an effort to transform an organization from performing ad hoc CSI activities to undertaking more formal and ongoing CSI activities, it is critical that participants and stakeholders are informed of all changes to the processes, activities, roles and responsibilities.

The goal of the communications plan is to gain support for the initiative, and build and maintain awareness, understanding and enthusiasm among stakeholders.

When developing a communication plan, it is important to realize that effective communication is not based solely on a one-way flow of information, and it requires more than just meetings. A communications plan must incorporate the ability to deal with responses and feedback from the targeted audiences.

The plan should include a role to:

- Design and deliver communications to the different CSI roles, stakeholders (such as other ITSM process roles) and identified target audiences
- Identify forums for customer and user feedback
- Receive and deliver responses and feedback to the project manager and/or process team members.

Key activities for the communications plan include:

- Identifying stakeholders and target audiences
- Developing communications strategies and tactics
- Identifying communication methods and techniques
- Developing the communications plan (a matrix of who, what, why, when, where and how)
- Identifying the project milestones and related communications requirements
- The tools and techniques to use to gain a perspective on the level of audience understanding, e.g. surveys, website hits, event participation etc.

In order to change behaviours and ultimately an organization's culture requires a well-thought-out communication strategy and plan. To be effective, this should focus on creating awareness of why the organization is implementing service management, why it wants to formalize a CSI process, and why ITIL was chosen as the best-practice framework. The plan will also need to address how to provide service management education through formal training programmes or internal meetings, how to provide formal training on the new processes and tools that sets new expectations, and how to provide updates on progress and achievements.

6.5.1 Defining a communication plan

In defining your plan, you need to take into consideration the following topics:

- **Who is the messenger?** This is often overlooked when assessing the importance of aligning the messenger with the messages.

- **What is the message?** Define the purpose and objective of the message, tailoring it to the target audience.
- **Who is the target audience?** The target audience for CSI could be senior management, mid-level managers or the staff who will be tasked with performing CSI activities. The target audience will dictate who will deliver the message, based on what the message is.
- **Timing and frequency of communication** Be sure to plan and execute your communication in a timely manner.
- **Method of communication** Sending emails and putting something on the web can work for some forms of communication, but in order to manage change effectively it is important to have a number of face-to-face meetings where there is an opportunity for two-way communications to take place.
- **Provide a feedback mechanism** Be sure to provide some method for employees to ask questions and provide feedback on the change initiative.

6.5.2 Communication transformation

The strategic management level usually initiates communication about new initiatives, and this should be true for implementing CSI within your organization. The CSI initiative is handed down from the strategic level to the tactical level and then to the operational level. Normally, each level goes through its own transformation process. It is important that the same message is being sent and received as the vision is communicated down the organization. The outcome of this process is the trigger, and often the demand, for the next level in an organization to transform.

What can also happen is that the content of the vision and reasons for the organizational change becomes less understood as the initiative moves down through the organization. Only parts of the rationale behind the organizational change come through to the operational level. Figure 6.1 shows how only part of the original content of the vision is handed down ('the shadow of the upper level') to the operational level. As the message is passed through the organizational levels, the clarity and content of the vision is blurred even further.

Figure 6.1 Vision becomes blurred

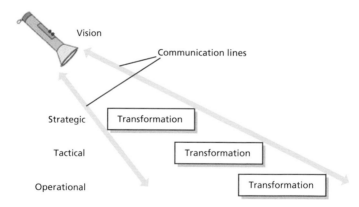

Because each management level has its own separate transformation processes, each level fails to appreciate the feelings of the other levels. This is most evident for operational level staff, who feel particularly vulnerable if they have not been involved in the discussions, yet the commitment and energy of operational level staff are essential to the success of any organizational change.

6.6   SUMMARY

Developing a governance structure is important for formalizing CSI in your organization. CSI will require that key roles are filled for trend evaluation, analysis reporting and decision-making. Process compliance is critical for ensuring that the proper output for process metrics is used for identifying process improvement initiatives. Technology will need to be in place for monitoring and reporting. Communication is critical to help change employees' behaviour. Communication will be necessary to identify the target audience, who the messenger is, what the message should be, and what is the best way to communicate that message.

7 Challenges, risks and critical success factors

7.1 CHALLENGES

There are many potential challenges to ensuring successful implementation of CSI activities, and these include:

- Managing necessary behaviour changes
- Ensuring that there are adequate tools
- Having the correct resources and the appropriate skills
- Lack of management commitment
- Inadequate resources, budget and time
- Lack of mature service management processes
- Lack of information, monitoring and measurements
- Lack of knowledge management
- Lack of corporate objectives, strategies, policies and business direction
- Lack of IT objectives, strategies and policies
- Lack of knowledge and appreciation of business impacts and priorities
- Resistance to change and cultural change
- Poor relationships and communication, and lack of cooperation between IT and the business
- Over-commitment of resources, with an associated inability to deliver (e.g. projects always late or over budget)
- Poor supplier management and/or poor supplier performance.

7.2   RISKS

These are some of the risks that may be faced:

- Being over-ambitious – do not try to improve everything at once; be realistic with timelines and expectations
- Not discussing improvement opportunities with the business – the business has to be involved in improvement decisions that will impact them
- Not focusing on improving both services and service management processes
- Not prioritizing improvement projects
- Implementing CSI with inadequate tools (or no tools at all)
- Implementing a CSI initiative with no resources – this means that people must be allocated and dedicated to this
- Implementing CSI without knowledge transfer and training
- Not performing all steps of the seven-step improvement process
- Making strategic, tactical or operational decisions not based on knowledge gained
- Management not taking action on recommended service improvement opportunities
- Not liaising with personnel in the business in order to understand new business requirements
- Failing to implement a communication/awareness campaign for an improvement (or implementing a campaign that is inadequate or late)
- Not involving the right people at all levels to plan, build, test and implement the improvement
- Removing testing before implementation or only partially testing; all aspects of the improvement (people, process and technology) must be tested, including the documentation.

7.3 CRITICAL SUCCESS FACTORS

The following are examples of critical success factors (CSFs):

- Appointing a CSI manager
- Adopting CSI within the organization
- Ensuring management commitment – ongoing, visible participation in CSI activities such as creating a vision for CSI, communicating the vision, direction-setting and decision-making, when appropriate
- Defining clear criteria for prioritizing improvement projects
- Adopting the service lifecycle approach
- Having sufficient and ongoing funding available for CSI activities
- Resource allocation – having people dedicated to the improvement effort, not as just another add-on to their already long list of tasks to perform
- Technology supporting the CSI activities
- Adopting processes – embracing service management processes instead of adapting them to suit personal needs and agendas.

8   Key messages and lessons

CSI requires a commitment from everyone in IT working throughout the service lifecycle to be successful at improving services and service management processes. It requires ongoing attention, a well-thought-out plan, consistent attention to monitoring, analysing and reporting results with an eye toward improvement. Improvements can be incremental in nature but also require a huge commitment to implement a new service or to meet new business requirements. Continual improvement should be embedded into all activities so that there is a constant search for a better way to deliver the services.

This key element guide has spelled out the seven steps of the CSI process. All seven steps need attention. There is no reward for taking a short cut or for not addressing each step in a sequential manner; if any step is missed, there is a risk of failing to meet the goals of CSI.

IT services must ensure that proper staffing and tools are identified and implemented to support CSI activities. It is also important to understand the difference between what should be measured and what can be measured. Start small – do not expect to measure everything at once. Understand the organizational capability to gather data and process the data. Be sure to spend time analysing data, as this is where the real value comes in. Without analysis of the data, there is no real opportunity to truly improve services or service management processes. Think through the strategy and plan for reporting and using data. Reporting is partly a marketing activity. It is important for IT to focus on the value added to the organization as well as reporting on issues and achievements. In order for steps five to seven to be carried out correctly, it is imperative that the target audience is considered when packaging the information.

An organization can find improvement opportunities throughout the entire service lifecycle. An IT organization does not need to wait until a service or service management process is transitioned into the operations area to begin identifying improvement opportunities.

Implementing CSI is not an easy task: it requires a change in management and staff attitudes and values to ensure that everyone understands continual service improvement is something that must be carried out if you are to succeed.

9   Related guidance

This chapter provides some information about other frameworks, best practices, models and quality systems that have synergy with the ITIL service lifecycle.

9.1   RISK ASSESSMENT AND MANAGEMENT

Risk may be defined as uncertainty of outcome, whether a positive opportunity or negative threat. Formal risk management enables better decision-making based on a sound understanding of risks and their likely impact.

A number of different methodologies, standards and frameworks have been developed for risk management. Each organization should determine the approach to risk management that is best suited to its needs and circumstances.

Approaches to risk management that should be considered include:

- Office of Government Commerce (2010). *Management of Risk: Guidance for Practitioners.* TSO, London.
- ISO 31000
- ISO/IEC 27001
- Risk IT[2]

9.2   ITIL GUIDANCE AND WEB SERVICES

ITIL is part of the Best Management Practice portfolio of best-practice guidance.

---

[2] With the publication of COBIT 5, Risk IT will be included within COBIT.

The Best Management Practice website (www.best-management-practice.com) includes news, reviews, case studies and white papers on ITIL and all other Best Management Practice guidance.

The ITIL official website (www.itil-officialsite.com) contains reliable, up-to-date information on ITIL – including information on accreditation and the ITIL software scheme for the endorsement of ITIL-based tools.

Details of the core ITIL publications are:

■ Cabinet Office (2011). *ITIL Service Strategy*. TSO, London.
■ Cabinet Office (2011). *ITIL Service Design*. TSO, London.
■ Cabinet Office (2011). *ITIL Service Transition*. TSO, London.
■ Cabinet Office (2011). *ITIL Service Operation*. TSO, London.
■ Cabinet Office (2011). *ITIL Continual Service Improvement*. TSO, London.

The full ITIL glossary, in English and other languages, can be accessed through the ITIL official site at:

www.itil-officialsite.com/InternationalActivities/TranslatedGlossaries.aspx

The full range of ITIL-derived and complementary publications can be found in the publications library of the Best Management Practice website at:

www.best-management-practice.com/Publications-Library/IT-Service-Management-ITIL/

9.3   QUALITY MANAGEMENT SYSTEM

Quality management focuses on product/service quality as well as the quality assurance and control of processes. Total Quality Management (TQM) is a methodology for managing continual improvement by using a quality management system.

ISO 9000:2005 describes the fundamentals of quality management systems that are applicable to all organizations which need to demonstrate their ability to consistently provide products that meet requirements. ISO 9001:2008 specifies generic requirements for a quality management system.

9.4   GOVERNANCE OF IT

ISO 9004 (Managing for the sustained success of an organization – a quality management approach) provides guidance on governance for the board and top management of an organization.

ISO/IEC 38500 is the standard for corporate governance of IT. The purpose of this standard is to promote effective, efficient and acceptable use of IT in all organizations.

9.5   COBIT

The Control OBjectives for Information and related Technology (COBIT) is a governance and control framework for IT management created by ISACA and the IT Governance Institute (ITGI).

COBIT is positioned at a high level, is driven by business requirements, covers the full range of IT activities, and concentrates on what should be achieved rather than how to achieve effective governance, management and control. ITIL provides an organization with best-practice guidance on how to manage and improve its processes to deliver high-quality, cost-effective IT services.

Further information about COBIT is available at www.isaca.org and www.itgi.org

9.6   ISO/IEC 20000 SERVICE MANAGEMENT SERIES

ISO/IEC 20000 is an internationally recognized standard for ITSM covering service providers who manage and deliver IT-enabled services to internal or external customers. ISO/IEC 20000-1 is aligned with other ISO management systems standards such as ISO 9001 and ISO/IEC 27001.

One of the most common routes for an organization to achieve the requirements of ISO/IEC 20000 is by adopting ITIL best practices.

Further details can be found at www.iso.org or www.isoiec20000certification.com

9.7   ENVIRONMENTAL MANAGEMENT AND GREEN/ SUSTAINABLE IT

'Green IT' refers to environmentally sustainable computing where the use and disposal of computers and printers are carried out in sustainable ways that do not have a negative impact on the environment.

The ISO 14001 series of standards for an environment management system is designed to assure internal and external stakeholders that the organization is an environmentally responsible organization.

Further details are available at www.iso.org

9.8 PROGRAMME AND PROJECT MANAGEMENT

The principles of programme management are key to delivering on time and within budget. Best management practice in this area is found in Managing Successful Programmes (MSP) (TSO, 2011).

Visit www.msp-officialsite.com for more information on MSP.

Portfolio, Programme and Project Offices (P3O) (TSO, 2008) is aimed at helping organizations to establish and maintain appropriate business support structures with proven roles and responsibilities.

Visit www.p3o-officialsite.com for more information on P3O.

Structured project management methods, such as PRINCE2 (PRojects IN Controlled Environments) (TSO, 2009) or the Project Management Body of Knowledge (PMBOK) developed by the Project Management Institute (PMI), can be used when improving IT services.

Visit www.prince-officialsite.com for more information on PRINCE2.

Visit www.pmi.org for more information on PMI and PMBOK.

9.9 SKILLS FRAMEWORK FOR THE INFORMATION AGE

The Skills Framework for the Information Age (SFIA) supports skills audit, planning future skill requirements, development programmes, standardization of job titles and functions, and resource allocation.

Visit www.sfia.org.uk for further details.

9.10 CARNEGIE MELLON: CMMI AND ESCM FRAMEWORK

The Capability Maturity Model Integration (CMMI) is a process improvement approach developed by the Software Engineering Institute (SEI) of Carnegie Mellon University. CMMI can be used to guide process improvement across a project, a division or an entire organization.

The eSourcing Capability Model for Service Providers (eSCM-SP) is a framework developed by ITSqc at Carnegie Mellon to improve the relationship between IT service providers and their customers.

For more information, see www.sei.cmu.edu/cmmi/

9.11 BALANCED SCORECARD

The balanced scorecard approach provides guidance for what companies should measure to provide a balanced view. The balanced scorecard suggests that the organization be viewed from four perspectives, and it is valuable to develop metrics, collect data and analyse the organization relative to each of these perspectives:

■ The learning and growth perspective
■ The business process perspective
■ The customer perspective
■ The financial perspective.

Further details are available through the balanced scorecard user community at www.scorecardsupport.com

9.12   SIX SIGMA

Six Sigma is a data-driven process improvement approach that supports continual improvement. The objective is to implement a measurement-oriented strategy focused on process improvement and defects reduction. A Six Sigma defect is defined as anything outside customer specifications.

There are two primary sub-methodologies within Six Sigma: DMAIC (Define, Measure, Analyse, Improve, Control) and DMADV (Define, Measure, Analyse, Design, Verify). DMAIC is an improvement method for existing processes for which performance does not meet expectations, or for which incremental improvements are desired. DMADV focuses on the creation of new processes.